found vol. II

BEACHCOMBING IN ORKNEY

KEITH ALLARDYCE

Published by The Orcadian Limited (Kirkwall Press)

Hell's Half Acre, Hatston, Kirkwall, Orkney, KW15 1GJ

Tel. 01856 879000 • Fax 01856 879001 • www.orcadian.co.uk

www.orcadian.co.uk/shop/index.php

ISBN 978-190295772-2

Printed in Orkney by The Orcadian, Hatston Print Centre,

Hell's Half Acre, Kirkwall, Orkney, Scotland, KW15 1GJ

Proceeds of the Royalties from *Found vol. II* will be donated to Stromness Museum

ACKNOWLEDGEMENTS by Keith Allardyce

With great patience, kindness and humour, many people have given me the privilege of taking their portraits, and of inquiring into their lives, during the journey around Orkney for this second volume of *Found*. This openness and warm hospitality continued even when an apparently 'instant' photograph can often be anything but instant. So my thanks go to all who appear in this book. And my thanks go to the generous people who simply helped in so many other ways on the journey.

My old friends are appreciated too – Bryce Wilson, Tom Muir and Doris Stout – who gave their support during this second volume's progress. This time around, Iku and I stayed with Tom in Kirkwall, where he always offered great hospitality, and where we met so many of his wide circle of friends… museum people, archaeologists, story-tellers, a screenwriter, a student, musicians… Tom seems to have become Orkney's ambassador.

And of course I must thank Iku, my partner, for her support and for her endurance throughout the *Found* project, as well as for her valuable creative and technical input, and for her patient editing of the photographs. And for holding the reflector even in the occasional gale.

Finally, I'd like to thank the team at The Orcadian in Kirkwall for their effort in the production of the two volumes of *Found*. But I must single out two people – one is Drew Kennedy, for pulling all the material together and designing the *Found* books with those illusive qualities, originality and simplicity. And the other is James Miller, for taking on the project in the first place, and for his encouragement. No sooner had I shown James the photographs for the original *Found* book than he said: 'There's bound to be more material out there for a second volume.'

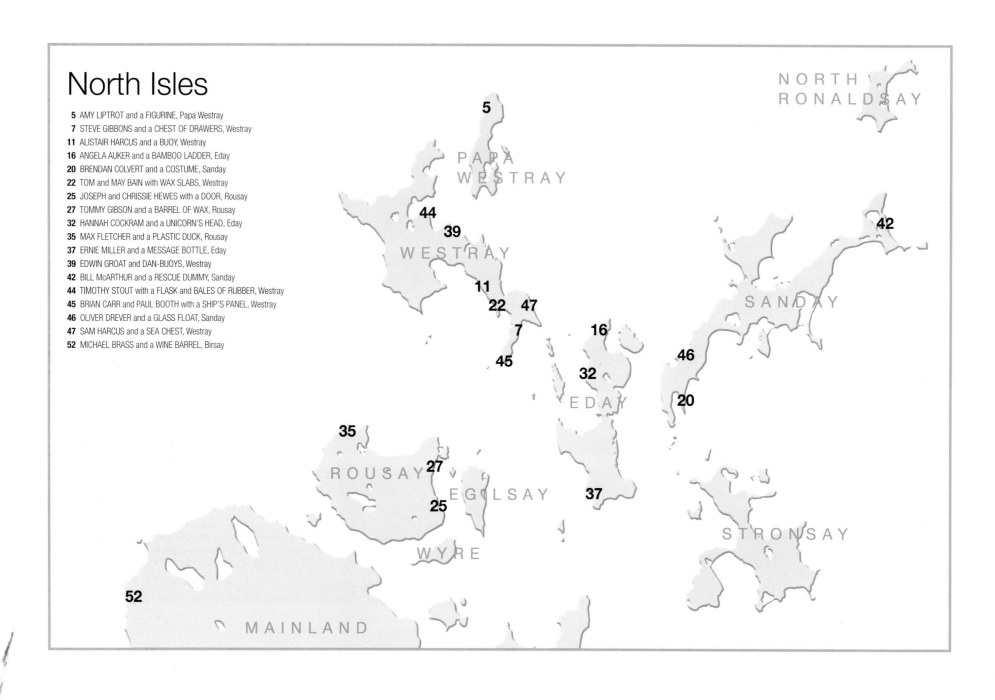

North Isles

5 AMY LIPTROT and a FIGURINE, Papa Westray

7 STEVE GIBBONS and a CHEST OF DRAWERS, Westray

11 ALISTAIR HARCUS and a BUOY, Westray

16 ANGELA AUKER and a BAMBOO LADDER, Eday

20 BRENDAN COLVERT and a COSTUME, Sanday

22 TOM and MAY BAIN with WAX SLABS, Westray

25 JOSEPH and CHRISSIE HEWES with a DOOR, Rousay

27 TOMMY GIBSON and a BARREL OF WAX, Rousay

32 HANNAH COCKRAM and a UNICORN'S HEAD, Eday

35 MAX FLETCHER and a PLASTIC DUCK, Rousay

37 ERNIE MILLER and a MESSAGE BOTTLE, Eday

39 EDWIN GROAT and DAN-BUOYS, Westray

42 BILL McARTHUR and a RESCUE DUMMY, Sanday

44 TIMOTHY STOUT with a FLASK and BALES OF RUBBER, Westray

45 BRIAN CARR and PAUL BOOTH with a SHIP'S PANEL, Westray

46 OLIVER DREVER and a GLASS FLOAT, Sanday

47 SAM HARCUS and a SEA CHEST, Westray

52 MICHAEL BRASS and a WINE BARREL, Birsay

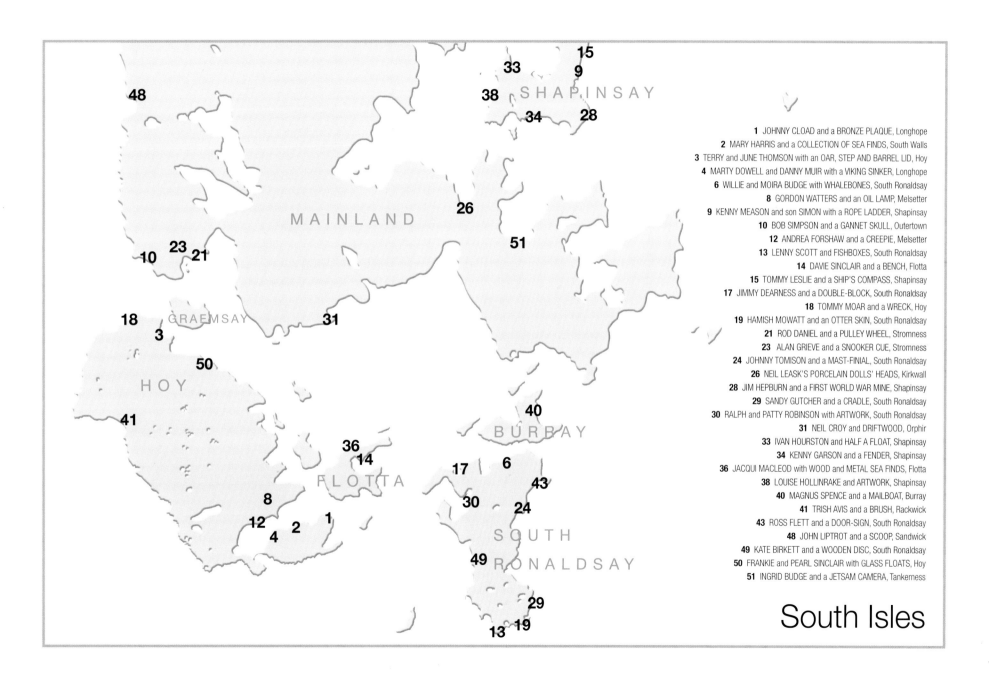

SHAPINSAY

MAINLAND

GRAEMSAY

HOY

FLOTTA

BURRAY

SOUTH RONALDSAY

South Isles

1 JOHNNY CLOAD and a BRONZE PLAQUE, Longhope
2 MARY HARRIS and a COLLECTION OF SEA FINDS, South Walls
3 TERRY and JUNE THOMSON with an OAR, STEP AND BARREL LID, Hoy
4 MARTY DOWELL and DANNY MUIR with a VIKING SINKER, Longhope
6 WILLIE and MOIRA BUDGE with WHALEBONES, South Ronaldsay
8 GORDON WATTERS and an OIL LAMP, Melsetter
9 KENNY MEASON and son SIMON with a ROPE LADDER, Shapinsay
10 BOB SIMPSON and a GANNET SKULL, Outertown
12 ANDREA FORSHAW and a CREEPIE, Melsetter
13 LENNY SCOTT and FISHBOXES, South Ronaldsay
14 DAVIE SINCLAIR and a BENCH, Flotta
15 TOMMY LESLIE and a SHIP'S COMPASS, Shapinsay
17 JIMMY DEARNESS and a DOUBLE-BLOCK, South Ronaldsay
18 TOMMY MOAR and a WRECK, Hoy
19 HAMISH MOWATT and an OTTER SKIN, South Ronaldsay
21 ROD DANIEL and a PULLEY WHEEL, Stromness
23 ALAN GRIEVE and a SNOOKER CUE, Stromness
24 JOHNNY TOMISON and a MAST-FINIAL, South Ronaldsay
26 NEIL LEASK'S PORCELAIN DOLLS' HEADS, Kirkwall
28 JIM HEPBURN and a FIRST WORLD WAR MINE, Shapinsay
29 SANDY GUTCHER and a CRADLE, South Ronaldsay
30 RALPH and PATTY ROBINSON with ARTWORK, South Ronaldsay
31 NEIL CROY and DRIFTWOOD, Orphir
33 IVAN HOURSTON and HALF A FLOAT, Shapinsay
34 KENNY GARSON and a FENDER, Shapinsay
36 JACQUI MACLEOD with WOOD and METAL SEA FINDS, Flotta
38 LOUISE HOLLINRAKE and ARTWORK, Shapinsay
40 MAGNUS SPENCE and a MAILBOAT, Burray
41 TRISH AVIS and a BRUSH, Rackwick
43 ROSS FLETT and a DOOR-SIGN, South Ronaldsay
48 JOHN LIPTROT and a SCOOP, Sandwick
49 KATE BIRKETT and a WOODEN DISC, South Ronaldsay
50 FRANKIE and PEARL SINCLAIR with GLASS FLOATS, Hoy
51 INGRID BUDGE and a JETSAM CAMERA, Tankerness

TREASURE

by Fiona MacInnes

What a droll pun

For the Atlantic to pull

Swirling among the flotsam

All the tales of things that were found

The treasures of the Sou-Westerly

Once it was a ship

With pianos for America

Plinkered among the stones

Spark plugs and pens and a

Cargo of toys...

Stories to widen my childish eyes

And now washed up a pallet of biscuits

Snug and sodden

Still in their tins

All over the shore for someone's tea party

Mermaid Butter Cookies

From *To Step Among Wrack* 1988, The Orkney Press.

INTRODUCTION by Bryce Wilson, author of *Stromness, a history*

The first edition of *Found* caught the public imagination and was soon sold out, leading to the reporting of many more interesting beach finds. With the encouragement of the publisher, Keith Allardyce set to work on a much-anticipated second edition.

Keith's photographs have an air of calm and dignity, but, be not deceived, for the photographic process is fraught with pitfalls and dangers of which I had first-hand acquaintance during work on the first edition. We would visit the island of Graemsay, the photographer bearing on his back a huge and weighty whale vertebra. At last we reached Geomarion on the western shore of the island, where the great whale had come ashore over a century before.

It was my turn to carry the burden. Seaweed and slippery stones negotiated, I was asked to climb and sit precariously upon a succession of ever-higher rock ledges, all the while balancing the heavy and increasingly awkward vertebra. "Try to look relaxed!" came the instruction. A couple of hours and many photo shots later, we were seated on the ferry, homeward bound. Keith was examining the results. "We'll have to try again next summer", came the verdict.

This new crop of photographs comes with tales of sea voyage and shipwreck, farmer and fisherman, beachcomber and artist, fleeting glimpses of island life caught and preserved by lens and laptop.

"...for Orkney lay athwart a great seaway from Viking times onward, and its lore is crowded with sailors, merchants, adventurers, pilgrims, smugglers, whalers, storms and sea-changes. The shores are strewn with wrack, jetsam, occasional treasure."

From *The Wreck of the Archangel* by George Mackay Brown

FOREWORD by Tom Muir

The first two weeks of January, 2015, saw storms that unleashed the full fury of the North Atlantic Ocean on Orkney's coastline. Huge breakers sent water crashing over the tops of high cliffs and pounding the shore like liquid fists. This is an age-old battle: the elements against the islands. On 2nd January, the cargo ship, *Cemfjord*, was lost in high seas to the east of the Pentland Firth with the loss of its eight-man crew; a terrible and shocking start to the New Year. It reminds us that the sea is an awesome force that should be treated with respect. In former times, the loss of a ship in a storm was not necessarily seen as a bad thing, as its wooden hull, sailcloth, ropes and cargo were salvaged by islanders who were in need of anything that the sea could provide. One person's misfortune was another person's good luck. Before we judge our ancestors by our modern standards, let us remember that there was little provision for the poor, elderly or sick in those days other than what the family could provide. A wreck could make the difference between a sickly child or an elderly person making it through a hard winter.

As the mountainous waves crash ashore, they disturb the seabed and carry in items long hidden in the ocean's depths. Wrecks on the seabed are disturbed, and robust pieces of their cargo can be dislodged and find their way ashore. There is no knowing what secrets the sea will bring to the beachcomber after a storm. A friend of mine recently found a strange tubular structure on the shore of Scapa Flow which looked very suspiciously like a torpedo. There was a good reason for that: it was a torpedo! Whether it was a practice one or a real one, I never heard, but it isn't as unlikely as it sounds when you remember that Scapa Flow was a major naval anchorage during both world wars. The fact that the torpedo lay undiscovered on the seabed for many decades suggests that it was a live one, as practice ones were designed to float so that they could be recovered later.

Whether floating on the waves or driven ashore from the depths by storms, the shoreline of Orkney is still a place where strange and exotic things may be found: from a bird skull to a Viking-age fisherman's weight, from floats and fish boxes to a carved piece of a sailing ship's hull. Many of these finds are turned into useful everyday items, or even into pieces of artwork. The partnership between the beachcomber and the sea provides a continuous link in the heritage of our islands. For as long as people have lived here they have searched the shoreline for the treasures that the sea is prepared to yield.

CONTENTS

1 JOHNNY CLOAD and a BRONZE PLAQUE, Longhope

2 MARY HARRIS and a COLLECTION OF SEA FINDS, South Walls

3 TERRY and JUNE THOMSON with an OAR, STEP AND BARREL LID, Hoy

4 MARTY DOWELL and DANNY MUIR with a VIKING SINKER, Longhope

5 AMY LIPTROT and a FIGURINE, Papa Westray

6 WILLIE and MOIRA BUDGE with WHALEBONES, South Ronaldsay

7 STEVE GIBBONS and a CHEST OF DRAWERS, Westray

8 GORDON WATTERS and an OIL LAMP, Melsetter

9 KENNY MEASON and son SIMON with a ROPE LADDER, Shapinsay

10 BOB SIMPSON and a GANNET SKULL, Outertown

11 ALISTAIR HARCUS and a BUOY, Westray

12 ANDREA FORSHAW and a CREEPIE, Melsetter

13 LENNY SCOTT and FISHBOXES, South Ronaldsay

14 DAVIE SINCLAIR and a BENCH, Flotta

15 TOMMY LESLIE and a SHIP'S COMPASS, Shapinsay

16 ANGELA AUKER and a BAMBOO LADDER, Eday

17 JIMMY DEARNESS and a DOUBLE-BLOCK, South Ronaldsay

18 TOMMY MOAR and a WRECK, Hoy

19 HAMISH MOWATT and an OTTER SKIN, South Ronaldsay

20 BRENDAN COLVERT and a COSTUME, Sanday

21 ROD DANIEL and a PULLEY WHEEL, Stromness

22 TOM and MAY BAIN with WAX SLABS, Westray

23 ALAN GRIEVE and a SNOOKER CUE, Stromness

24 JOHNNY TOMISON and a MAST FINIAL, South Ronaldsay

25 JOSEPH and CHRISSIE HEWES with a DOOR, Rousay

26 NEIL LEASK'S PORCELAIN DOLLS' HEADS, Kirkwall

27 TOMMY GIBSON and a BARREL OF WAX, Rousay

28 JIM HEPBURN and a FIRST WORLD WAR MINE, Shapinsay

29 SANDY GUTCHER and a CRADLE, South Ronaldsay

30 RALPH and PATTY ROBINSON with ARTWORK, South Ronaldsay

31 NEIL CROY and DRIFTWOOD, Orphir

32 HANNAH COCKRAM and a UNICORN'S HEAD, Eday

33 IVAN HOURSTON and HALF A FLOAT, Shapinsay

34 KENNY GARSON and a FENDER, Shapinsay

35 MAX FLETCHER and a PLASTIC DUCK, Rousay

36 JACQUI MACLEOD with WOOD and METAL SEA FINDS, Flotta

37 ERNIE MILLER and a MESSAGE BOTTLE, Eday

38 LOUISE HOLLINRAKE and ARTWORK, Shapinsay

39 EDWIN GROAT and DAN BUOYS, Westray

40 MAGNUS SPENCE and a MAILBOAT, Burray

41 TRISH AVIS and a BRUSH, Rackwick

42 BILL McARTHUR and a RESCUE DUMMY, Sanday

43 ROSS FLETT and a DOOR SIGN, South Ronaldsay

44 TIMOTHY STOUT with a FLASK and BALES OF RUBBER, Westray

45 BRIAN CARR and PAUL BOOTH with a SHIP'S PANEL, Westray

46 OLIVER DREVER and a GLASS FLOAT, Sanday

47 SAM HARCUS and a SEA CHEST, Westray

48 JOHN LIPTROT and a SCOOP, Sandwick

49 KATE BIRKETT and a WOODEN DISC, South Ronaldsay

50 FRANKIE and PEARL SINCLAIR with GLASS FLOATS, Hoy

51 INGRID BUDGE and a JETSAM CAMERA, Tankerness

52 MICHAEL BRASS and a WINE BARREL, Birsay

1

JOHNNY CLOAD and a PLAQUE, South Walls

Photographed near his home at the Martello Tower and Battery at Hackness, in South Walls, Johnny Cload holds a bronze plaque depicting the Egyptian goddess Isis. This handsome trophy was found on the shore near the tower during the Second World War.

'It was attached to the broken stern of a lifeboat – it was from HMS *Isis*, a destroyer,' said Johnny. Battling through Switha Sound during a heavy sea, the destroyer took a pounding when one of its lifeboats was wrenched from its position on board and wrecked. Kept for decades by Johnny as a souvenir, after his father had informed the Receiver of Wrecks at the time, the plaque has recently been given to the Scapa Flow Visitor Centre.

As it was about two years into the war before Johnny received his call up papers, he saw the rapid development of the naval base and the arrival of thousands of forces personnel at Lyness, near his home. He witnessed, for example, the first terrifying Lufftwaffe air raids on Scapa Flow, and he heard the colossal blast when the *Royal Oak* blew up following Commander Prien's U-boat attack.

On joining the Royal Engineers in late 1941, Johnny served in North Africa, on the way surviving an Italian attack which sank his ship. By the end of the war, he was serving in Greece. Back in Orkney, he took on his family's small-holding at the Martello Tower. It's where his grandfather served as an artillery man, was a caretaker there in the early 20th century, and finally bought the property from the War Department. For many years, Johnny served as a guide to the tower and battery; he also found earlier employment labouring at Lyness, and as a roadman for the council. Awarded the Africa Medal, and the MBE, Johnny celebrated his ninety-fourth birthday on 13th September, 2014, and is Hoy's oldest resident.

MARY HARRIS and a COLLECTION OF FINDS, South Walls

Dedicated beachcomber Mary Harris lives near the shore of Longhope Bay. Cropping up frequently on Facebook's 'Beachcombing in Orkney' page, news of Mary's finds is shared with many other beachcombing enthusiasts. And so a visit was arranged. Mary's territory was a major centre of activity as a naval base during two world wars, and interesting objects connected to that time frequently appear on the shore.

'Sea Cottage', Mary's home in Longhope, overflows with sea finds. Deep window-sills display rows of fascinating objects… a raven's skull, sculptural bones, glassware, the back of a chair (like a lyre), buttons, and even a range of old wooden toothbrushes, and more finds whose purpose remain a mystery. The complete skeleton of a porpoise hangs on a wall, two typographers' trays hold more treasure, and a long piece of wood has been sliced to reveal the busy pattern of shipworm holes.

Outside are even more finds, and in a shed… 'And there's a boundary stone,' says Mary, 'from the shore, conveniently carved with the letter M for Mary… or it might be Melsetter.'

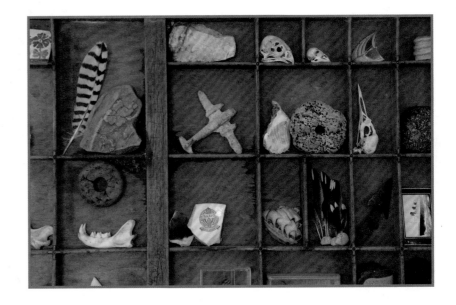

TERRY and JUNE THOMSON with an OAR, STEP and BARREL LID, Hoy

'The Bu was a major farm in Viking times, and could have been the headquarters of a Viking area manager, or the captain of a longship… and the room we're in,' said Terry Thomson, 'was built in 1164 – that's recorded, and it could be earlier.' I had called on Terry and June at their home, the Bu of Hoy, after meeting two of their neighbours, Frankie and Pearl Sinclair, a mile or two down the road. 'They'll be worth a visit,' said Frankie, and that's how it was, neighbour recommending neighbour.

'There's a skeleton of a smuggler under the floor,' said Terry in a matter-of-fact way, as we talked and drank mugs of tea, '…and he's lying just under where you're sitting… shot during an argument, sometime in the 17th century…' 'But on to beachcombing,' I said, shuffling my feet, 'you must have found a few things here…' The Bu stands beside the Bay of Creekland on Burra Sound, opposite Graemsay – perfectly sheltered from the westerly gales. Outside, we looked around the farmyard and the outbuildings. There was so much, and I selected a step and a barrel lid. Then Terry appeared from a byre with a very long yole oar, which June's mother had found about thirty years earlier.

It didn't matter what the objects were. They had been found on the shore, and considered worthy of collecting… perfect additions for a portrait… and in the background, the great rise of Hoy's Ward Hill.

MARTY DOWELL and DANNY MUIR with a SINKER, South Walls

This Viking-era sinker is made of steatite, sometimes called soapstone, and was found by Marty Dowell on the Cantick shore, in South Walls. Living there at the time, Marty and one of his mates, Danny Muir, were both keen beachcombers, and were photographed where the sinker was found in 2012.

I asked Danny's father, Tom Muir, about the sinker. He said 'It's definitely a Viking/medieval line sinker. Only one was found in the whole of Quoygrew, none at Pool – they're not so common in Orkney, though two were found on the Brough of Birsay. Most common in Late Norse rather than Viking, it was quite likely made in Shetland, though they do get found in Norway.'

On double-checking the sinker's age with Paul Sharman, Senior Projects Manager of the Orkney Research Centre for Archaeology (he specialises in steatite artefacts), Tom found that he considered the sinker to be 'Late Norse, or medieval, depending on whose terminology you're following. The 12th to 15th centuries were when they were most common, though could be earlier, could be later.'

AMY LIPTROT and a PORCELAIN FIGURINE, Papa Westray

Night listener, sea swimmer, diarist. Just three activities listed in her Twitter account, Amy Liptrot is otherwise a writer and journalist. In 2016, her book *The Outrun*, a memoir, will be published by Canongate.

Responding to a letter I placed in *The Orcadian* appealing for people to let me know about their beachcombing finds, Amy sent me an email: 'My favourite thing I've found,' she wrote, 'is probably this headless, footless, handless figurine – at South Wick on Papay (where I'm living at the moment). Someone told me that it might have come from a wrecked ship that was carrying porcelain figurines!'

During the last two summers, Amy Liptrot has been roaming some of the islands at night, listening for corncrakes. These rare birds are secretive and nocturnal and, fortunately for the survey, are very vocal. As the Orkney RSPB Corncrake Initiative Officer, Amy is otherwise known as 'the corncrake wife.'

Perhaps Amy's main interest is sea swimming, and therefore she might know the coast of Orkney more intimately than most. Meeting for a dip once a week throughout the year with a small band of hardy folk known as the Orkney Polar Bear Club, Amy has become a true sea sprite.

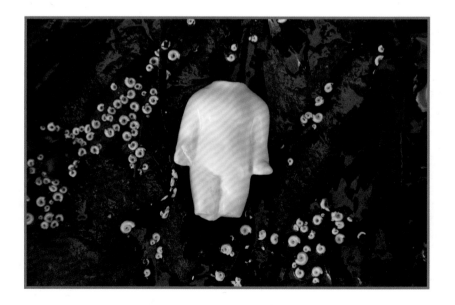

WILLIE and MOIRA BUDGE with WHALEBONES, South Ronaldsay

In the seaside graveyard of St. Peter's Church, on the south-east coast of South Ronaldsay, there stands a small memorial stone, quite different from any other. Designed and carved by Willie Budge, the stone depicts a ship, with only the stern-half above the ground. And then you notice the keel… it's cleverly carved as a face, and there are two hands together in prayer.

The stone is in memory of two crew members of the mv *Joanna Thorden*. On her maiden voyage from Helsinki to New York and back (she was on her return voyage), the vessel struck the Pentland Skerries in a storm in 1937. Half of the crew, plus the captain's wife and small son, and the wife and small son of the engineer, were put into a lifeboat. It was later found capsized at Dingieshowe, with a man's body nearby. One of the women's bodies was washed up at Lopness Bay, Sanday, but the rest were never recovered.

The *Joanna Thorden* broke in two, and the bow section drifted on to Swona. Just before it broke in two completely, the captain ordered "abandon ship", and the remaining crew took to the ship's second lifeboat. Steering through rough seas towards St. Peter's Kirk, the boat was capsized about half a mile offshore, where the seabed shelves upwards. Two of the men drowned here were buried in the kirkyard, and their graves are maked by two small stone slabs; the other bodies were returned to Finland for burial.) Willie Budge

took it upon himself to commemorate the two men with this beautiful memorial, and its haunting simplicity, a work of art, expresses a mood of deep pathos.

In this portrait with his wife Moira, another side of Willie Budge's character is revealed. The strange, curving string of whales' vertebrae is a piece of sculptural whimsy. (It's made from the bones of three whales.) And beside a barn lies what could be Orkney's biggest pile of whalebones, collected by Willie over the last three or more decades.

7 **STEVE GIBBONS and a CHEST of DRAWERS, Westray**

I knew this had to be followed up. Discovering a Facebook alias of 'Hershel Vankidneybeans', and news of a beachcombing find of a complete chest of drawers, I made a note of the name. Then following my appeal in *The Orcadian* for news of beachcombing finds, I heard from Hershel himself : 'I'm just reading *The Orcadian* and I thought I'd send you a photo of what I think must be my best find…. The frame was separated from the drawers, but I found every piece scattered over maybe 500 metres of shoreline… it has the name Jaden on it.'

A few weeks later, I was on the Westray ferry to photograph Steve with his find. Meeting me at the pier with his 1985 ex-Birmingham taxi, we tried a few photographs on the Sands of Woo, where the chest was found. Two men lifting out of a taxi a chest of drawers, and taking it along a beach to sit it down at the water's edge – we must have made an unusual sight. But in a very contrasty light, and a dull background, we abandoned the location for an attempt at Steve's house. There I found the perfect setting – a background of beachcombing paraphernalia (and a dog, my favourite prop).

GORDON WATTERS and an OIL LAMP, Melsetter

Before moving to Orkney, Gordon Watters lived in the most remote part of the Scottish mainland, the Knoydart peninsula. His house was near the shore of Loch Hourn, and access was only by sea. It was in this spectacular and dramatic scenery that Gordon fished for prawns and white fish in his 25ft trawler.

After moving to Orkney in 1976, he found work as a farmhand. But he's not a landlubber. Enquiring about any vacancies on the *Hoy Head* in Scapa Flow, he was taken on as a cook/deckhand on the Houton-Lyness-Flotta circuit. Four years later, he was skipper of the ferry – and he's still the skipper, 'Thirty-four years and six months on,' Gordon told me.

The oil lamp Gordon is holding in this photograph was found in January, 1932, when the Grimsby trawler, *Dorby*, was wrecked at Tor Ness – it's a notorious part of the Hoy coast. People gathered on the shore near the wreck - and they helped three of the trawler's crew reach safety after the stricken fishermen jumped into the sea. The remaining eight were rescued by the Longhope lifeboat. And somehow, amongst the wreckage on the shore, this lamp from the *Dorby* survived intact - and many years later the man who found the lamp gave it to Gordon.

9

KENNY MEASON and son SIMON with a ROPE LADDER, Shapinsay

'It's a pilot's ladder,' said Kenny Meason, 'and someone's forgotton to haul it up the side of a ship after a pilot has visited.' The ladder was found by Kenny in the Bay of Crook, near his Frustigarth cattle farm on Shapinsay's north-east coast. There have been Measons farming here since the mid-17th century and, now that Kenny has retired, he's handed over the running of the farm to his son, Simon, and his family.

Ideally placed to be involved with research into the problems facing seal populations around the Scottish coast, Kenny Meason was until recently one of the Sea Mammal Research Unit's 'Seal Team'. Operating from the Scottish Oceans Institute, based in St Andrews University, the team has eight members who work with their director, Silje-Kristin Jensen. Biotoxins are a factor in the decline in populations of harbour seals, and Kenny has contributed to research by regularly collecting scat for the Scotland team looking into seal diet.

BOB SIMPSON and a GANNET SKULL, Outertown

A couple of miles out of Stromness – I'm with Bob Simpson on the shore at Breckness. It's a perfect location for beachcombing, catching the Gulf Stream as it pours through Hoy Sound on the tide and continues east into Scapa Flow. Bob's holding a sun-bleached gannet skull in this photograph. The bird could have been hatched on Sule Stack, a great lump of a rock about forty miles west of Orkney. Over 5,000 pairs of gannets breed on the island every summer. From Suleskerry, the Stack's near neighbour, I've seen them as I peered through the lighthouse telescope – a great, swirling white cloud of seabirds around a white rock, between a dark green sea and a pale blue sky – an extraordinary, impressionist, round image.

Drawn to Orkney from Dorset in 1990, Bob's interest in nature ranges from birds to moths, and he records all his findings. 'I've always been interested in the wildlife around me,' he remarked, 'especially along the shore. But then I started to look at the rubbish I was seeing on these walks.' Curiosity led Bob to discover that the thousands of plastic shotgun cartridges which are washed up every winter in Orkney are in the wake of wildfowling on the east coast of North America. 'And plastic coloured tags in their thousands come here too – they can be traced to Newfoundland by their code numbers,' said Bob, 'and then there are plastic bottles from all over the world.'

Bob loves these islands, and he summed up his endless fascination with Orkney in a reflective mood: 'The islands and the strand line hold so many mysteries and there's so much to see, from the power of a screaming gale to a nice night watching the Merry Dancers flickering in the north.'

ALISTAIR HARCUS and a BUOY, Westray

Living just above the shore of the Bay of Cubbigeo, Alistair and June Harcus run a cattle and sheep farm on Westray's southern limb. June was born in Eday. 'I'm an island person, and I love it,' she said with enthusiasm. 'I like the space and the air… and you're part of the community,' June continued. 'I walk on the shore with the grandchildren these days… they're keen to find things. There was a bottle message from the Faroe Islands…'

The buoy in this photograph was found by Alistair floating around in the Bay of Tafts, a couple of miles along the coast from his house, in 2006. Alistair had been out creeling when he found the buoy and towed it ashore. It was a marker buoy for a salmon farm which was once based in the area. The cage never contained fish – it was only being tested, but the company was later wound up.

'I tried to sell the buoy on eBay,' said Alistair, but there were no bidders, and so it has remained above the shore near his house, like an extraordinary monument, or a fountain needing to be plugged into a water supply.

ANDREA FORSHAW and a CREEPIE, Melsetter

Made from Canadian red pine, which she found on the North Bay shore near her home, this wooden stool held by Andrea Forshaw has been made in the traditional Orkney fashion. 'Orcadians call them creepies… this one has a lovely, deep colour, and a fine grain,' Andrea said. 'And I've made a few more. One was made from wood, which I'm told could have come from the *Joanna Thorden*. It has lettering "Reserved for Use of Crew" incised by hand in a 1930s' Eric Gill-ish typescript.'

Andrea has never had to travel far to discover shore finds. Apart from the Canadian driftwood, in 2010 she spotted a tiny glass bead, less than a centimetre in diameter, sparkling cobalt blue on a gravel beach near her house. 'It could have come from an eroded tomb just above the shore,' said Andrea. First introduced into Britain by the Romans, glass beads were later highly prized by the Vikings, who used them along their trading routes across Western Europe, from Iceland to the Caspian Sea.

As part of Hoy's Melsetter estate, Andrea's home was originally a flax mill, and stands close to the North Bay shore. Nearby, the estate's Melsetter House is the country's finest example of Arts and Crafts Movement architecture. It is the laird's house, a magnificent and fascinating building, and was designed by William Lethaby, a friend of the movement's pioneer, William Morris. 'Simple but honest was Lethaby's theme,' said Andrea. And while the architect was working on Melsetter House in the 1890s, he also worked on converting the mill into a house.

LENNY SCOTT and FISHBOXES, South Ronaldsay

I rang Lenny Scott soon after returning to Northumberland in early September – 'We've had two days of storms from the south-east,' he said, 'and the barriers were closed for two days.' The Pentland Firth was in a wild state, with waves crashing on the cliffs beyond Lenny's house, and sending spray 200 feet and more into the sky and lashing the fields half a mile inland.

Running a farm at Cleat, in the deep south of South Ronaldsay – 'We've got cattle and suckler coos here,' Lenny said, 'and we grow our own silage.' In earlier years, Lenny was a stonemason, building houses, byres, sheds, walls… and farming alongside too. There was always time for beachcombing – collecting fishing floats (pictured); and fishboxes were always useful. 'If you found them you took them home,' he said, 'useful for storing seed tatties, tools, anything…'

Lenny was a member of the South Ronaldsay Coastguard at the time of the Longhope lifeboat disaster on the night of 17th March, 1969. The lifeboat *TGB* capsized after setting out from Longhope to assist a cargo ship, the SS *Irene*, adrift in a fierce storm and mountainous seas. The following day, the lifeboat was found floating upside down in the Pentland Firth. All eight of the crew lost their lives that terrible night. The *Irene* was later beached on the east side of South Ronaldsay.

'There were twenty of us in the rescue of the *Irene* crew,' said Lenny, 'and we had the Deerness Coastguard with us. It was a night of storms and hailstones. It wasn't a bonny night. Our searchlights lit up the ship. Seventeen were taken off, and then taken to Kirkwall… they were put on a plane and flown out of Orkney early the next morning.'

DAVIE SINCLAIR and a BENCH, Flotta

Flotta has its own ambassador – this man is a husband, father, sub-postmaster, shop keeper, raconteur, humourist, a community councillor off and on, tour guide (he's known for spontaneously giving visitors to Flotta a trip around the island), and a founding member of the Flotta Heritage Trust. He is Mr Flotta.

To more serious things, Davie is also a founding member of the 'crack team' known as the Flotta Freedom Fighters, who are still 'ready to spring into action' if necessary. His alter ego is well known as Willock o' Pirliebraes – and two hilarious books have been written about this extraordinary character. (Recommended reading – *Willock o' Pirliebraes* and *Willock and the Black, Black Oil*, published by The Orkney Press.)

Davie's website is also worth a read – he covers a wide range of topics, including the time when Occidental Oil Inc. established an oil terminal in Flotta : '…in 1974 I was in the right place at the right time to make a pound or two off the oil company and yet be a nuisance to them and the local authority when, in my view, they stepped out of line.'

About the bench in this photograph – 'I don't see it coming from a trawler,' said Davie, 'and I don't really know where it came from.' I took a few photographs as we talked. 'It has PORT marked on one side. I'm inclined to think it's from a sailing ship', he said, 'but it's a bit of a mystery.'

TOMMY LESLIE and a SHIP'S COMPASS, Shapinsay

Iku and I knocked on the door at 'Hillside', a farmhouse overlooking the Firth of Stronsay. The old, faded red door opened, and Tommy Leslie listened to my request. As we talked, his mother popped her head around an inner door, curious to see what the strangers wanted. In no time we were made welcome, while Tommy thought about what might interest us.

Taking a small box from a dark, dusty corner in one of his barns, Tommy slid open the lid to reveal this beautiful compass in pristine condition. 'My father was a boy at the time when he found the compass,' he said, 'and he'd have been a hundred years old by now.'

The compass originally belonged to a Norwegian schooner, wrecked on Westray. 'Being in a box, the compass would have been on the ship's lifeboat… for an emergency… the skipper might have given it away as a keepsake,' said Tommy.

Tommy's mother and father lived on a six-acre croft in Westray before moving to the island of Faray for seven years. Then the move to Shapinsay followed, to take on, to start with, forty-eight acres. Tommy has carried on with the farm, with more acreage now, and has always creeled too. The long, dark winter nights are the time for making straw-back chairs, both the frames and the straw-work. 'The most I've made in one

season is four,' said Tommy, as he showed us his workshop. Then another interesting object, too beautiful to pass by, was drawn from a dark corner - a large, decorated mast finial, with weathered paintwork of gold and red, found by Tommy's uncle on the Shapinsay shore.

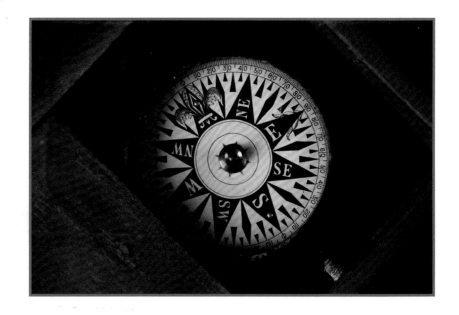

ANGELA AUKER and a BAMBOO LADDER, Eday

Standing on a piece of Eday's red sandstone, Angela Auker holds a bamboo ladder she found on the island's east coast in 2012.

'I had to rescue the ladder from a bonfire – my husband was having a clear-out,' said Angela, 'but I never use the ladder. It's just a bit special. It could be from Japan, after the tsunami…' The ladder is ten feet in length, and tapers slightly towards the top. It has nine rungs, all made of bamboo. Even the pegs which keep the rungs positioned are made of bamboo, each one having a neatly-cut square head.

Having decided to move from Scarborough to live in Orkney in 2010, Angela arrived by yacht with her husband Ivan. They sailed in a clockwise direction around Britain, and eventually passed through the Hebrides, rounded Cape Wrath, and, because of the wrong tide for Stromness, anchored in the tiny harbour of Tingwall, opposite Rousay. The next day, Angela and Ivan sailed for Eday, an island they had set their hearts on, mainly for the excellent sub-aqua diving possibilities around the island. Tying up at the pier after the great adventure, all seemed well for a day or two. But then a gale suddenly blew up, making the boat vulnerable in its exposed berth – Angela and Ivan's arrival in Eday became a baptism by storm, so they made a dash for Kirkwall to find a safe harbour.

Since this unconventional but exciting arrival in Orkney, Angela and Ivan have been renovating a cottage in Eday. On their days off, diving around the Eday coast means collecting scallops (a good barter currency, says Angela), photographing the beautiful marine life, and exploring the wreck of a First World War Admiralty tug, the *Oceana*, which sank following a collision with a trawler in October, 1918.

JIMMY DEARNESS and a DOUBLE-BLOCK, South Ronaldsay

Photographed for this book at the age of 93, Jimmy Dearness is at home on the Hoxa peninsula, where he has farmed all his working life. We'd met sixteen years earlier – when I photographed Jimmy with his son on the balcony at Hoxa Head Lighthouse, for *Scotland's Edge Revisited*. Having just retired from his position as Attendant Keeper, Jimmy handed over the reins to his son, Jimmy. (Jimmy senior and his wife Alice have one son and nine daughters.)

'Have you anything you've found on the shore?' I asked Jimmy. I was convinced there'd be an interesting object here. But the answer was no. But cups of tea and scones were on the way, and a little later Jimmy said he'd got a collection of about two hundred fishboxes… all collected from the shore, and stacked in the barn. With tea over, and with Jean, one of Jimmy's daughters over from Flotta, we went to have a look in the barn. It was all a bit tidy, with a couple of large pieces of farm machinery and a yole, and the neatly stacked 'wall' of fishboxes. But then I noticed on a shelf a double-block, a piece of a sailing ship's rigging. 'Did this come from the shore, Jimmy?' I asked, when we returned to the house - and, possibly just to keep me happy, he assured me it was indeed from the shore.

Photographed in her Kirkwall workshop, Katrina Bews uses sea glass and beach stones in a creative and an imaginative way to make decorations for the town's 'The Studio Shop'. Even making her own wedding bouquet out of a string of dog whelks: 'it did have additions of silk here and there to make it prettier,' she added. On the bench in front of Katrina is a sailing ship's rigging block, found on Scapa beach after a great storm. On drying, even slowly, the block suddenly cracked open to reveal an abstract design, a piece of sculpture.

18

TOMMY MOAR and a WRECK, Hoy

This is not quite a beachcombing 'find' but I thought it worthy of inclusion in the book. On the night of Thursday, 24th October, 1952, the Aberdeen steam trawler *Strathelliot* ran aground in a severe south-easterly gale on rocks at Selwick, Hoy's most northerly point. The vessel must have been huge – it had a crew of twelve, and the massive boiler, twelve feet in diameter, still survives unmoved on the wreck site.

The story of the rescue that night is an unusual one, so I was keen to go out to the wreck at low tide to photograph it. And to make it even more worthwhile, Tommy Moar, the farmer who lives in sight of the wreck, and who witnessed the dramatic rescue of the *Strathelliot's* crew six decades earlier, agreed to go out too.

There was no loss of life during the *Strathelliot* drama, though it involved the longest breeches-buoy rescue in history. The distance between the wreck and the shore was 360 metres.

The Orkney Herald reported 'For six hours during Thursday night and Friday morning, in wild conditions, the Longhope life-saving apparatus company worked to take all twelve members of the *Strathelliot* off by breeches buoy.' However, the following Tuesday, the skipper and two of his crew were back on board the stricken trawler, trying to arrange for it to be refloated, when another gale suddenly blew up and left them stranded. The breeches-buoy crew went into action yet again, this time joined by the Stromness Lifesaving Company, and the three men were once more returned to dry land. A total of thirty men had taken part in the *Strathelliot* rescue episode. As he left for Aberdeen and home, the skipper George Simpson told *The Orcadian* 'I shall never forget the kindness of the Orkney people.'

19

HAMISH MOWATT and an OTTER SKIN, South Ronaldsay

Driving as far south in Orkney as it's possible to go, Iku and I reached Banks on the southern tip of South Ronaldsay. Further south still lie the Pentland Skerries, almost three miles distant. There is a modern bistro at Banks, run by Hamish Mowatt and Carole Fletcher – and the diners have perfect views of the Skerries while they enjoy lobster and crab, and scallops and halibut... Hamish was photographed at the bistro, beside an otter skin on the wall. He found the dead animal on the shore nearby in 2010 - at about the same time that he discovered a Neolithic tomb next to the bistro. Named 'The Tomb of the Otters', because of evidence of otter activity and otter bones in the tomb, human remains still lie within.

And, with that view of the Pentland Skerries and its lighthouse, looking so near, and framed by the bistro windows, memories of two weeks of light-keeping came flooding back for me and my time there, just a little: a fall of goldcrests before these tiny birds departed on their journey across the North Sea to Scandanavia; reading the Shipwreck Return Book, and learning about bravery and disaster in hand-written accounts by former Principal Light Keepers going back nearly two centuries – one I still remember, of the wreck of the schooner *Good Desire* in 1871, 'the man drifted away on the tide... the Attending Boatman never seed anything of the man that drifted past the island on the boat's bottom'; listening on an old valve radio in my bedroom to a distress call from a couple on a storm-bound yacht between Scotland and Norway, as in terror they spoke to Stonehaven Coastguard; and peering into a strange funnel in the middle of Muckle Skerry, yet connected to the sea – Walter Scott described this feature in his 1814 journal 'when the tide is high, the waves rise up through this aperture in the middle of the isle – like the blowing of a whale in noise and appearance.' And the loneliest, and one of the saddest graves in Scotland, where, on a stone plaque set into a wall, is written 'In memory of nine of the crew of the *Vicksburg* of Leith, seven of whom lie buried here July 17th 1884. Also two children of P.Reid PLK 1872 - 1879.'

20

BRENDAN COLVERT and a COSTUME, Sanday

We are sitting in the huge kitchen of Stove, a grand mid-19th century farmhouse at the head of the Bay of Stove. There is Earl Grey tea, and smart fishbox shelving for small sea finds, a thick bench of mahogany from a Start Point wreck, and paintings and cards fill spaces all around the room.

Brendan Colvert and Rosey Priestman are concerned with trying to keep the house in good repair, and with sculpting and painting. And with visitors who come to stay. 'They bring their kids,' says Rosey, 'and they love it.' The rooms are full of surprises and intrigue. One room had some huge canvases with work in progress, and Brendan picked up a weird piece of sculpture he found on the shore – it was expanded polystyrene which had been released from its spray-can while floating in the sea… ready-made modern art.

'The first object I found on the shore here was a plastic hard-hat,' said Brendan, 'and it was engraved like scrimshaw with drawings of birds and fish.' Having gathered a large collection of buoys in those early years, two fishermen arrived one day 'and bought them for forty pounds and a trout,' said Brendan, and added, ' we were hard up, so we were really happy about that.'

Near the house, the high tide reaches to a low embankment. On the ebb, the tide drains the bay, and the sea can be half a mile away. Opportunities abound for beachcombers here. The costume which Brendan is wearing in this photograph consists entirely of objects found on the shore - the jacket and trousers, gloves and boots. Dolphin skulls hang from the jacket. The mask is a cow's pelvis.

21

ROD DANIEL and a PULLEY WHEEL, Stromness

Rod Daniel is photographed here holding a sea-worn souvenir which he found on the shore below his Stromness waterfront house. The object has had three decades of sculpting by the sea. The oak interior has an iron rim, fragile and rusty.

Like so many beachcombing finds, this object, with its unique form, colour and texture, has become a piece of modern art. But it began its life as a pulley wheel, driving a conveyor belt in the town's Stockan's Bakery. The business originally had its base on the site where Rod's house now stands. Around the time of the bakery closing in the 1990s, when the business moved to bigger premises, some parts of the building's machinery ended up in the harbour. Ever since, unusual pieces of iron and wood occasionally appear on the shore, and, if they're not collected by a beachcomber, they somehow disappear into the depths again.

Rod Daniel is a consultant opthalmologist at London's Moorfields Eye Hospital. Commuting from Stromness to the Capital, working alternate fortnights, works well for him, and will continue until retirement. He and his wife live in a remarkable modern house, which fits with great subtlety within the traditional architecture of the town. This year, the Orkney-based architect commissioned to design the house, Shane Scott, received a Saltire Society Housing Design Award for the building. Occasionally, when Rod looks at the shore from a high window, something catches his eye. A small collection is accumulating…

22

TOM and MAY BAIN and WAX SLABS, Westray

The fate of the MV *Joanna Thorden*, the 5,000-ton ship which foundered in the Pentland Firth in hurricane-force winds in 1937, has featured before in the pages of this and the first volume of *Found*. Twenty-five of its crew and passengers were lost. Bodies and pieces of the ship's cargo were washed up on South Ronaldsay and many other Orkney islands.

The wax which Tom and May Bain are holding was found thirty or more years ago. 'They'd come ashore in sacks,' said Tom, 'four blocks to a sack. They came from the *Joanna Thorden*, that's what's thought, and they always came ashore here after south-easterly gales.' May continued: 'The wax was useful as a fire-lighter… to start a driftwood fire to boil pots of tatties for our pigs and hens. And our youngest son used to make candles out of the wax.'

In 2012, Tom found a kayak on the shore near their farm on Westray's southern tip. Having informed the Coastguard about the kayak, he learned that it had been lost two weeks earlier in Skye. The kayaker had been in difficulties, when he was separated from the kayak. He survived, but was in distress because it belonged to his boss.

23 ALAN GRIEVE and a SNOOKER CUE, Stromness

On its way from Hamburg to Sydney, the three-masted schooner *Edenmore* ran aground off Stronsay on 7th October, 1909. All of the 25-man crew were saved, and its cargo was 'saved' too… it was 'well looted by the islanders' (according to a marine archaeology report), having on board chinaware, furniture, chemicals and machinery, 23 pianos and 23,000 slates.

'Many of those slates were sold and used in Stromness… there'll still be houses in the town with *Edenmore* slates,' said Alan Grieve. There will no doubt be other traces of the *Edenmore's* cargo around Orkney – plates and teapots, a sideboard, chairs… perhaps even some of the pianos were salvaged, and still being played somewhere in the islands.

Alan meets with a few friends to play snooker a couple of times a week, in his converted garage, using a cue from the *Edenmore*. In sharp contrast to Alan's childhood home at Fa'Doon, a seventeen-acre croft in Rousay, there's plenty of space around the home he shares with his wife Connie on the outskirts of Stromness. The Fa'Doon crew consisted of Alan and his sister, their mother and father, an aunt and uncle and their two children, and two grandparents.

24

JOHNNY TOMISON and a MAST FINIAL, South Ronaldsay

I'd just photographed Ross Flett on the clifftop near his house, when he pointed to someone on the shore. 'That's my neighbour, Johnny Tomison, he'll have found something,' said Ross, 'he's often beachcombing.'

Half an hour later …'This is from the top of a ship's mast,' said Johnny, in his sitting-room. The window light was perfect for a portrait. 'And here's something made by an Italian prisoner of war,' he said, as he handed me a wooden carving of the Madonna, an incredibly beautiful work of art about six inches in height, and made with astonishing, flowing lines, yet with careful detail. 'The Italians had been working on the Churchill Barriers, of course,' said Johnny, 'and the carving had originally been given to my uncle… he was carting concrete blocks from Holm for the construction of the barriers at the time.'

We had a look around together outside for more finds. 'The first thing I ever found,' said Johnny, 'was a wooden clog, years ago. Then I found a leather football.' More recently, Johnny picked up a small plastic disc, an inch and a half in diameter. 'The disc was one of four million which had been accidentally released from a sewage works in the States,' he said. Behind Johnny's house stood a large capstan, its origins unknown, but it had been used by his father for winching fishing boats up the shore near St. Peter's Church.

In an abandoned house next door to Johnny, a room was crammed with doors and panels removed from a pirate ship – of the modern variety. It was called the MV *Comunicator,* and was well-known as a radio station called Lazer 558, broadcasting pop music from the North Sea in the 1980s. But the station was short-lived, and after the ship was bought and sold in subsequent years by a variety of radio stations, it was finally used by Superstation, which broadcast to Orkney until 2004. The ship now lies near St. Margaret's Hope and will be broken up for scrap metal.

25

JOSEPH and CHRISSIE HEWES and a BILGE BOARD, Rousay

'It's sometimes quite watery around here!' said Chrissie Hewes, at Nethermill, the cottage she is renovating with her artist husband, Joseph. The sea reaches up to the garden dyke just metres below the house. And, with a south-easterly blowing, the garden can be full of seawater. Then, along one side of the house, there is the mill burn – the mill itself above Nethermill is now disused – while at the other side of the house runs the Sourin Burn. Heavy rains bring the burns to a spate with a roar.

But, with a view across Rousay Sound from Nethermill to the island of Egilsay, the watery world in all its moods around Joseph and Chrissie's home is part of the charm and the drama of the place. Egilsay is the island where Magnus Erlendsson, Orkney's St Magnus, was betrayed by his cousin Earl Haakon. Magnus was murdered. As George Mackay Brown wrote, 'Then in the light of a new day, 16th April 1117, there was a blinding flash of metal in the sun.'

With the sea on their doorstep, Joseph and Chrissie occasionally pick up useful jetsam. The door in this photograph was found on the shore. It was originally a boat's bilge board, boat-shaped in outline. So the length and sides were trimmed to fit a doorframe. 'And those blue propcorn bins are washed up too,' said Chrissie. 'They're useful for trimming to size to make flower containers.'

26

NEIL LEASK'S PORCELAIN DOLLS' HEADS, The dolls' heads came from Westray - though Neil lives in Kirkwall

When the sailing ship *Travancore* left Hull on 13th February, 1871, bound for New Orleans, she headed straight into a series of violent storms. The vessel's sails were soon in tatters, and she became waterlogged. On reaching the east side of Orkney, and unable to attempt an Atlantic crossing, the master, Captain Flett, decided to drive the stricken ship on to the safety of the soft beaches of Sanday. But the wind and the treacherous island currents swept the helpless *Travancore* and its terror-stricken crew westwards instead, where she was wrecked on Spo Ness, a rocky headland in Westray. Remarkably, there was no loss of life.

The *Travancore's* cargo was saved, and an auction organised later the next month in Westray attracted a lot of interest. The SS *Orcadia* brought many prospective bidders from all over Orkney. Two ships eventually took one thousand tons of railway iron from the *Travancore* on to their original destination, New Orleans, while the collection of sails, ropes, blocks, oars, anchors, three small boats and many other materials were all sold locally.

Though not listed in the sale announcement, there was a collection of porcelain dolls' heads in the auction. Believed to be from the *Travancore*, the dolls' heads in this photograph now belong to Neil Leask, well-known custodian of Corrigall Farm Museum and Kirbuster Museum. Neil was given the dolls' heads by his aunt, who in turn was given them by her next-door neighbour, Maggie Rendall, whose family came from Westray.

27

TOMMY GIBSON and a BARREL of WAX, Rousay

This photograph shows Tommy Gibson chipping off a lump of wax for me – I later melted this souvenir to make half-a-dozen candles. On the first day of meeting Tommy, and asking about finds – 'No, there's nothing I can think of…' The second day, 'Sorry, no… can't think of anything.' Later the same day: 'There might be…' On the third day, 'We'll have a look, there just might be something…'

Found on a Stronsay shore by Tommy Gibson's brother-in-law, this is one of several barrels of wax which were scattered around the Orkney Islands in the late 1930s. The wax came from the *Joanna Thorden*, a ship which was wrecked on her maiden return voyage from New York to Finland, when she foundered in the Pentland Firth in 1937.

The wax is barrel-shaped, the barrel itself having broken apart in the ship's hold or in the open sea. Having found it, Tommy's brother-in-law took it home. 'He then decided to send it to Rousay,' said Tommy. 'First it was put on to the ferry to Kirkwall, then it went by road to Tingwall, before travelling to Rousay. On the way, someone cut a hole in the top of the wax, and put a short, thick piece of rope in it – the biggest candle…'

This is a rare photograph of Tommy in his store which was originally a smithy near the island's pier. Ironic, really – as Tommy has a collection of almost forty cameras. The oldest is a neat little box – a 1920 Kodak Baby Hawkeye. And he has a collection of around 9,000 early photographs of life in Rousay. Tommy is a fount of information for Rousay exiles seeking their roots.

28

JIM HEPBURN and a FIRST WORLD WAR MINE, Shapinsay

There's a fairy-tale castle on Shapinsay, just up from the ferry terminal, and a neat row of houses forms the main street of the harbour village. There's a petrol station, and, in the heritage centre a café is run by volunteers who prepare fresh scones and tasty meals.

Someone told me about a string of farms which I could visit – along the arrow-straight road of Shapinsay's north-east corner – where there could be sea finds of interest. Names were mentioned… Meason, Tait, Hepburn, Leslie. I imagined ancient sheds and stores. I looked at the map and headed for Kirkton. Turning on to the farm drive, I saw the mine – and immediately thought the book wouldn't be complete without one.

'The mine was found by a man called Mainland,' Jim Hepburn explained, 'on the shore below Steenso, the farm next door. It was during the First World War, and after it was defused it was dragged up to the farm.' But then Steenso was put up for sale, and all the machinery, all the contents of the farm, were sold. Jim's grandfather bought the mine 'for a song', and put it where it stands today.

Jim was eighty-six years of age when this photograph was taken. He farmed at Kirkton all his working life. He started at the age of fourteen with his grandfather, just when his father tragically died after being injured by a bull.

29

SANDY GUTCHER and a CRADLE, South Ronaldsay

'There must be something…', said Sandy Gutcher, as we looked around his farmyard and barns for beachcombing treasure. His family have been here for many generations, in a house overlooking the Pentland Firth. Planks of wood are stacked for possible future needs. Dark, cavernous barns reek of mystery and the sea… Muckle Skerry and the Pentland Skerries Lighthouse lie almost due south of Sandy's farm. It was on the lighthouse supply boat, a unique Burray-built yole, that I first met Sandy and his five-man crew in the early 1980s – a memorable adventure in the Pentland Firth.

In one of the barns, almost full to the gunwales with sea finds, we made our way deep into its shadowy interior. On one wall hung part of a ship's bench – the curved, amber back about ten feet in length. 'I dragged that up the highest cliff in South Ronaldsay.' It was from the *Kathe Neiderkirchner,* a ship from Cuba which hit the Skerries in dense fog in 1965.

And then, looking up at the rafters, Sandy said, 'There's a cradle - it's been sitting there for seventy years … and I was the last person to use it.' By now, Sandy's son had arrived with a ladder, and we took the cradle out into the sunshine. 'This is the first time I've seen it doon,' said Sandy. The cradle had been found on the shore, and had been handed down with the story through the generations. 'I know it was in use before 1730,' he said, '…we throw nothing away here.'

30

RALPH and PATTY ROBINSON and ARTWORK, South Ronaldsay

Stopping on the road to Herston, the magical village strung along the southern shore of Widewall Bay, Iku and I had a chance encounter with Ralph Robinson, which led to our discovery of a fascinating art collection. And some of the art was very pertinent to the *Found* project. These occasional encounters were an important part of our exploration across Orkney, and they gave the project a great element of surprise.

We soon met Ralph's wife, Patty, and saw examples of her exquisite art, including a powerful image, a lino cut of two figures in black-and-white, and a series of more delicate, autobiographical drypoint prints. And then, in one room, there was a series of twenty-two pieces of Ralph's art. 'They are pieces of political art,' Ralph explained, 'and the collection is called Allochthon: Allegories of Migration.' The word 'allochthon' is a geological term to describe a stone that is found in a place other than where it was formed. Within each frame there is a painted driftwood background, and pieces of beachcombed china inlaid – both materials being found in a place other than their origin. 'A combination of spontaneity and serendipity brought us to Orkney in search of a home nearly thirty years ago', continued Ralph, 'so we, too, could be considered allochthons.'

Ralph's art was produced in a rage, a protest, at the derogatory use in some European countries of the term 'allochthon' to describe citizens of non-western descent. The pictures present an opposite view to the notion that the 'allochthon' migrants are a blemish on a nation state – rather, they represent the 'aliens' or 'incomers' adorning a nation's culture, and adding to the nation's fabric of character and spirit.

In a house, on an island off the north coast of Scotland, on the very edge of Europe, Ralph's pictures hang in silence and with great dignity. They represent something which the world needs urgently. Ralph, with Patty, said what they wanted to say with eloquence, and stood for a portrait. It was a poignant moment. It expressed in a quiet yet profound way so much about the best qualities of humanity.

31

NEIL CROY and DRIFTWOOD, Orphir

At Outer Dale, Neil Croy's farm above Swanbister Bay in Orphir, a dozen hen-houses are scattered here and there – it's a glimpse of how the Orkney landscape might have looked at the height of the islands' egg industry in the 1950s. 'The hens,' said Neil, 'that's what made the farm here.' But today only four of the hen-houses are in use – Neil's farming now revolves around one hundred cattle.

I photographed Neil beside bales of hay behind his house. A piece of fishing-net, recently found in Swanbister Bay, neatly secured the bales from the ravages of winter storms. When I asked about any more finds from the shore, Neil suggested having a look in a byre. 'It's just down the road,' he said, 'I've got another farm there.' 'You've got two farms?' I said. Neil replied, 'Well, I've got three farms around here!' In the byre, a soft light flowed through the doorway. The woodwork in the byre, all of it found on the shore, and heavily worn by cattle for more than a century, glowed with a rich golden colour. Another portrait was taken. 'The farms keep me busy,' said Neil, 'so there's no spare time… I've never been out of Orkney, never off the Mainland… never had an interest in going over the water.'

The farmhouse near this byre is where Neil was born. It's now used as a barn for the cattle's winter hay. 'We'd go for a walk along the shore most Sunday afternoons when I was a child,' said Neil, 'after church, after lunch… We found plenty of fire-wood, and a ladder,' he said. 'The ladder's been used ever since it was found in 1946… mainly early on when we built stacks with sheaves.'

32

HANNAH COCKRAM and a UNICORN'S HEAD, Eday

Found by the late Jimmy Shearer, a crofter on Eday's west side, this wooden carving of a unicorn's head is held by eight-year-old Hannah Cockram. (Hannah attends the island school of eight pupils.) The origins of the unicorn carving are a mystery, but Hannah's mother Kate thought it could have been a decoration on a boat. The carving is now on show in Eday's Heritage Centre.

Kate Townsend and her partner Adam Cockram are involved with Orkney Micro Renewables – it's a Community Interest Company 'dedicated to the belief that access to affordable renewable energy should be available to everyone.' Their tall wind turbine stands on the moor just behind Kate and Adam's house at Newbigging; off-shore there is an EMEC (European Marine Energy Centre) under water test turbine, and Adam is contracted to regularly monitor the site for its effects on wildlife.

Other facets to Kate and Adam's life in Eday include attending the island's airfield, otherwise called London Airport, as passenger attendants and firefighters, when the inter-island planes arrive and depart. They are also members of the Eday Fire and Rescue Service.

33

IVAN HOURSTON and half a FLOAT, Shapinsay

While compiling this book, I interviewed and photographed many intriguing people but none more so than Ivan Hourston from Shapinsay. Unfortunately for me, I soon discovered he wasn't a beachcomber but we had such an interesting time with him, I was desperate to include him in the book … somehow!

On restoring a dinghy, which had been damaged in Orkney's great storm of January, 1953, he became inspired. He was thirty-five years of age, and decided to give up his life as a farm labourer and a summertime lobster fisherman. He was to become a full-time boatbuilder.

Before his retirement, Ivan had built 160 boats. They ranged from small dinghies to 36-feet-long fishing boats. From his own designs, which he kept in his head, the smaller boats took shape; for the bigger boats he drew his own plans. Never needing to advertise, Ivan's skills were broadcast by word of mouth, and his boats are all around Orkney and the coast of Scotland. (He built, for example, fourteen 16ft boats with inboard diesel engines for Alginate Industries of the Western Isles.)

Meeting Ivan at his home in a former Shapinsay school, I was keen to take a portrait with a beachcombing find. 'Have you anything you found on the shore?' I asked. I was disappointed when he replied with a convincing 'nothing at all.' There were plenty of sheds, the sort which look as though they could have a few shore finds, but Ivan assured me there was nothing. 'Did you find an old flag?' I asked. 'No.' 'How about a small wooden object of any sort…?' 'No, nothing…I was never really a beachcomber,' he said. A little later, we had a look around, mainly to see the three boats Ivan had in the yard and the sheds. And suddenly I noticed something… we had entered the former dining room of the school… a small aluminium float which had been cut in half, on a shelf… and that was it…I'd found the key, the only object from the shore. The portrait could now be taken… with Ivan standing between one of his dinghies and two 50-year old Fordson Majors he had restored.

Talking to Ivan about his remarkable skill in boatbuilding, he said 'Making boats, you have something to look at… and many you never see again. When you finish a boat, every last detail, and it looks beautiful, it's sold and then the boat leaves… it's an emotional time… it's like losing an old friend.'

34

KENNY GARSON and a FENDER, Shapinsay

Photographed near the shore at his Shapinsay farm of Waltness, Kenny Garson is holding a fender which he found in 1998. Occasionally on the shore with his dog, he has a chance to keep an eye open for jetsam. The fender would have been lost from a yacht – it has a practical purpose, but has been made to look beautiful. It's a piece of modern art.

Kenny has now retired from farming, and, like most islanders, weaves into his life a number of community commitments. A self-taught accordionist, he plays in the island band at dances, weddings, the Lunch Club, and many other gatherings. He served in the island Fire Service for twenty-five years, and also recently retired from driving the ambulance. He contributes to the annual island show, and has been president of the National Farmers' Union.

Commuting between Shapinsay and Kirkwall for the last dozen years, Kenny's wife Sheila is a social history curator at the Orkney Museum. 'I'm more of a committee person than Kenny,' says Sheila, being involved with the Community Council, and the Development Trust off and on, and the Church of Scotland.

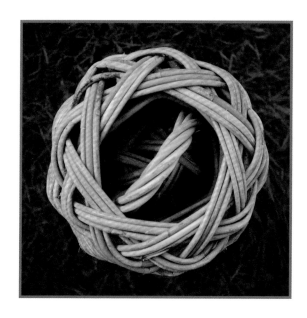

35 MAX FLETCHER and a PLASTIC DUCK, Rousay

A fundraising stunt involving 150,000 plastic ducks – all thrown into the River Liffey, in the heart of Dublin – was organised by a group of ten friends in aid of Our Lady's Hospital for Sick Children, Crumlin. The city's Today FM radio station sponsored the event, a world-record attempt duck race, along a one-kilometre stretch of the river, on 3rd June, 2006.

A large net across the Liffey succeeded in capturing all the ducks at the end of the race – but some mischievous children, when they had the chance, couldn't resist throwing some of the ducks back into the water. Two years later, in Rousay's Saviskaill Bay, Max Fletcher found one of those escapees, the duck's colour by then much faded – but its Irish origins could be traced through a faint, but still-legible, email address printed on its base. 'Some journey,' said Max. 'It turned left into the Irish Sea, and headed north to pass through The Minch… then around Cape Wrath and east along the Pentland Firth to Rousay.'

'I'm often on the shore,' Max told me, 'looking for anything useful… and I do a clean-up occasionally, picking up rubbish.' Around the year 2000, Max left behind his life as a press photographer, based in Portsmouth, to live on Rousay's western flank, on the very edge of Quendale, the site of George William Traill's clearance of the crofting community to make way for sheep, early in the 19th century.

36

JACQUI MACLEOD with WOOD and METAL FINDS, Flotta

Part-time postwoman Jacqui Macleod has just taken charge of the island's first Post Office van. 'It's a very old one,' said Jacqui, 'but on a good, sunny day I still do the round on my bike… it's about eight miles. It takes twice as long to do the round on a warm day, when people are out and there's time to meet and talk,' Jacqui remarked.

In this portrait, Jacqui is holding a piece of iron and wood from a ship. It's from the Flotta shore, which still yields objects from the First and Second World Wars. The top of a piece of curled steel (on the left in this photograph) was also collected from the shore, and it's part of the anchoring system of a barrage balloon. (There were nineteen barrage balloons over Flotta during the Second World War to protect the Scapa Flow naval base.) In the garden, there is a large axle from a wartime truck, which transported goods, mostly ammunition, from ships to shore bases.

Jacqui recently attended the island's Harvest Home, where around sixty people, many from the Orkney Mainland, celebrated and danced until the early hours. And on another day she explored a more remote part of the island, and counted about two-hundred seal pups on the shore. Flotta is fascinating, and it's one of Orkney's best kept secrets. (And Davie Sinclair didn't tell me to write that.)

37

ERNIE MILLER and a MESSAGE-BOTTLE, Eday

One of the most unusual message bottles found on the Orkney shore is probably Ernie Miller's, which he picked up one day late in 1954 – on Eday's Sealskerry Bay. He was a young farmer at the time, but always had time for beachcombing. Ernie removed from the bottle a small certificate. It was from the Guinness Company: 'The purpose of this 'Drop' was to help our Research Department in their efforts to ascertain perfect sealing of our product…. But, being human, (in the year of Our Lord 1954) the signer could not resist the temptation of using the opportunity by mentioning something about the health-giving virtues of Guinness Stout…' On informing the company of his find, Ernie received a silver teaspoon complete with a tiny, enamel Guinness bottle design on its arm.

Sarah Poutch of the Guinness Company's Archive Department in Dublin told me the story behind Ernie's bottle find. It was one of 50,000 dropped into the Atlantic, Pacific and Indian oceans – and Ernie's was dropped from the MV *Assyria* of the Cunard Steamship Company on 2nd July, 1954, off the coast of Labrador.

A subsequent advertising scheme marked the 200th anniversary of the Guinness Company in 1959, when 150,000 message bottles were dropped into the world's oceans – long before the 'Over the Side is Over' campaign. The brainchild behind the message-bottle campaign was the Liverpool-based managing director of Guinness Exports, AW Fawcett. He obviously had a sense of humour and a head brimming with ideas. Sarah Poutch told me her favourite Fawcett quote – 'A mad thought? Maybe – but all original thoughts are mad; and all thoughts have got to be made to work, but the madder the thought the harder the work.'

38

LOUISE HOLLINRAKE and an ARTWORK, Shapinsay

It's November, and I'm talking to Louise Hollinrake at her home on Shapinsay's west side. The terns which nested on the nearby Ayre have already departed south to the Antarctic. Now, on the little loch behind the Ayre, there are over sixty whooper swans – it's their first resting place as they migrate from the frozen north. 'It only takes them nine hours to reach us… they come from Iceland,' Louise commented, 'and there have been as many as a hundred and seventy on the loch.'

On a window-sill in Louise's sittingroom there are beachcombing finds from all over the world – shells, bird skulls, and a collarbone of a small whale. 'I've always been a beachcomber,' said Louise. 'I've always collected bruck… and I'm loathe to part with any of it.' There's a view, as special as any in Orkney, from this room. Between Shapinsay and its neighbours to the west, Rousay and Gairsay, there is a handful of skerries and holms, each with their own character. Seals haul out on one of them in big numbers. Another is a breeding ground of the charming tystie, the black guillemot.

Moving from Cumbria to Shapinsay in 1986, Louise chose the island to live in because it's smaller than most, and it's close to Kirkwall and the Orkney Mainland. 'The island is an entity, and therefore everyone has something in common… and the community was, and still is, welcoming.'

39

EDWIN GROAT and DAN-BUOYS, Westray

'We'd pick them up… for no reason. They were just floating around…a flag and a float, and a heavy lead weight underwater,' said Edwin Groat in his Pierowall home in Westray. 'But you find a use for things sometimes,' he said. And so it was with a handful of Edwin's dan-buoys, which are now used as clothes poles in his back garden. The dan-buoys, he said, would break away from the Danish and Norwegian boats, when he was creeling around the Westray coast.

Before taking to the Westray waters, Edwin was sailing around the Far East, Australia and New Zealand. 'I'm a Merchant man,' he said, 'and I've got some memories. I was on a ship on its way to New York from Liverpool; I was only 18 at the time… there was fog all the way across the Atlantic. It was July, 1956. We got a message that there had been a collision between two ships as we approached Brooklyn. There was debris and oil all over the sea. We heard that two sisters had been on the *Andrea Doria* and, with the impact of the collision, one of the sisters had been flung on to another ship, the *Stockholm*, and she survived. Her sister, who stayed on the original ship, was drowned. And then the fog suddenly cleared… and there was New York all around us… the sky-scrapers, the Hudson River, the Statue of Liberty.'

Back home in Orkney, Edwin was in Papay, Westray's next-door island, to attend a wedding. At the dance that evening, one girl caught his eye more than anyone else. The revelry petered out by around four in the morning, and, when the sun was already rising, Edwin asked if he could walk her home. 'Of course you can,' she said with a smile, and so the two meandered along the road, refreshed by the cool air. But on nearing her home, the girl suddenly announced 'Well, Edwin, I must put the ducks away – to make them lay in the morning…good night…' 'I was dismissed!' said Edwin.

However, Edwin wasn't dismissed for long. He again met the girl, Dorothy, who had caught his attention, when he was back in Papay a couple of weeks later. And, after a courtship of almost four years, they were married on a wild day of blustery winds and heavy snow showers in Papay's St. Ann's Church, on 27th March, 1968.

40

MAGNUS SPENCE and a MAILBOAT, Burray

Well-known in Orkney for his 'Orkan Adventures' holiday trips, Magnus Spence is also known as the man who saved a whale. From his boat in Scapa Flow, in 2012, he noticed a whale, its great back rolling over the sea, and the tail slowly rising and falling. But, on getting closer, he realised that the huge animal (it was a humpback whale) was in distress.

Diving into the sea to take a closer look, Magnus found that a discarded creel line was tangled around the whale's lower jaw, confining the unfortunate animal to a slow death, alternately rising to the surface to breathe, only to be dragged, exhausted, to the seabed by the heavy weight. Within a few minutes, Magnus cut the offending ropes from the whale, when it slowly swam away, free from its suffering.

While in Scapa Flow, providing another 'Orkan Adventures' trip, Magnus spotted a small white box on a remote beach. It turned out to be a St. Kilda-type mailboat, from Shetland, and was part of a campaign by CURE (Communities United for Rural Education) to publicise the threatened closure of six secondary school departments in the islands.

————

(Inset) Nick Gould's St. Kilda mailboat was put into the sea off St. Kilda by a work party on the island (the boat is named after Annette Sheppard, a work party leader). It was found by Nick and his wife Fiona in 1987, during a walk along the Rousay shore. In a small tin on the boat's deck were found a £5 note and some postcards, with a request to post them.

Less than a year after this portrait was taken in his beloved library at Fealquoy, his home overlooking Rousay's wide Saviskaill Bay and the North Isles, on 21st November, 2012, Nick passed away. 'Nick had been a journalist,' Fiona told me, 'but he was a true polymath. And he loved Orkney.' Iku and I were moved to read a copy of the funeral service. It included beautiful poetry by Robert Rendall, and *Hildaland* by Walter Traill Dennison, and quotations by William Morris; and an Old Norse proverb, 'The man who walks his own road, walks alone.'

At Wasbister Kirkyard, just below Fealquoy, Nick lies at rest. It's a beautiful graveyard, 'overlooking the sea and the sky which he loved so much.'

41

TRISH AVIS and a BRUSH, Longhope

Moving from Loughborough to Orkney with her husband around 2004, Trish Avis now lives in Longhope. Her former Leicestershire home was about as far from the sea as it's possible to live in England, but now Trish has a passion for the coast, beachcombing – and for PU3P and 'Bagging the Bruck'. Her husband Steve is also connected to the sea now – he's a cook/deckhand and relief mate on the *Hoy Head*, the ferry which runs between Lyness and Houton.

With Mary Harris, Trish regularly explores the island's shore, and they have an impressive collection of sea finds. The sweeping brush was found in 2013 in Rackwick Bay, and Trish put it in the bothy, a small and basic hostel, which sits just above the shore. 'I left it in the bothy to encourage the people who stay there to sweep up after them,' said Trish, 'and I didn't want to carry it with me – I was on a walk to the Old Man of Hoy with some friends at the time.'

Trish is photographed sitting on a boulder at Rackwick. Behind her, in a soft haze, stand the spectacular Hoy hills and cliffs. In his poem *Rackwick: A Child's Scrapbook*, George Mackay Brown wrote 'Hills tell old stories. Cliffs are poets with harps.'

42

BILL McARTHUR and a RESCUE DUMMY, Sanday

Standby rescue ships of the North Sea oil industry are fitted with semi-rigid nets designed for scooping up survivors when, for example, helicopters have ditched into the sea. Frequent rescue practices with these nets are made using dummies – they're tricky operations, and in rough seas it's inevitable some dummies are lost. Bill McArthur's rescue dummy, dragged from the shore, is used here as a scarecrow near his vegetable patch.

On entering his studio, I found Bill looking at an oil painting he'd been working on – a powerful wave, a wild sea. Around the walls hung more seascapes – impressions of storms, light and texture, and references to rocks and headlands – all showing subtle brushstrokes of those blues and greens and whites which can only come from people who know the sea.

Having graduated from Edinburgh College of Art in 1963, Bill became an art director at J. Walter Thompson in London. Returning to Edinburgh to run a silk-screen printing company, he continued there until deciding to sell the business – when he bought a fishing boat and moved with his family to Sanday.

During his twenty years as a commercial fisherman, Bill McArthur ranged from the far reaches of the North Sea to the west of the Hebrides, even as far as St Kilda and Rockall – and whenever possible he observed the changing qualities of water, light and sky.

43

ROSS FLETT and a SHIP'S DOOR SIGN, South Ronaldsay

The most poignant object in Ross Flett's possession was this small brass sign – it was originally attached to a piece of wood – and it was found on the shore near the wreck of the *Irene*. This is the ship, Liberian-registered and Greek-owned, which ran out of fuel while passing through the Pentland Firth in a terrible storm and mountainous seas on the night of 17th March,1969.

The Longhope lifeboat was called out to assist the vessel. But the sea conditions were so extreme, even by Orkney standards, that the lifeboat overturned and all eight men on board lost their lives. Shortly after this devastating tragedy, the *Irene* came to rest on the east coast of South Ronaldsay, not far from Ross's home, and the crew were safely taken off by breeches-buoy.

Ross Flett is well-known in the islands for running the charity Orkney Seal Rescue, and he was a co-founder of the Dunters, an Orkney environmental concern group – established initially to campaign against a proposal to open a massive uranium mine behind Stromness in the late 1970s. It was one of these early volunteers in the Dunters who established Orkney's 'Bag the Bruck' scheme, where people collect rubbish from the islands' beaches every spring.

Iku and I drove down the steep track to Ross's house, having been told he'd be worth a visit. A short-eared owl, golden in the clear light, watched us from a fence-post. It's a spectacular location. George Mackay Brown wrote about the place in one of his weekly *Under Brinkie's Brae* articles for *The Orcadian*, in 1976 – he was visiting Nora Kennedy, his muse, who lived there at the time. 'At last, there the cottage was, halfway down a wide fertile slope, rich that day with two immense fields of changing barley.' After describing a delicious meal with wine, which left them with 'dreaming heads', GMB wrote 'Afterwards we walked down to one of the most beautiful small beaches in Orkney. It curves, a golden-grey crescent… The sea that breaks on it is green and cold and translucent.'

44

TIMOTHY STOUT with a FLASK and RUBBER BALES, Westray

Sitting on one of two rubber bales he found in 2004 on the Westray shore, Timothy Stout is photographed at his caravan home in Pierowall. (He also found the useable flask he's holding.)

For a few years, Timothy and his family lived in Wick, and it was during that time that he found about ninety bales of rubber washed up on the coast. They came from a ship which sank ten miles off Wick in the 1970s. Many more were found by others at the time, and all the bales were transported south by road for sale and processing.

In Westray, Timothy also found a salmon-cage frame, which he sold to a company which uses it now on Lambholm (the Italian Chapel island) for rearing lobsters before release into Orkney waters. And it was back in Westray that Timothy took up creeling for a living, starting with a 10-feet-long dinghy. He progressed to a 17ft yole, then up to a 30ft former Auskerry Lighthouse supply boat, and finally a 36ft boat, newly built for Timothy at James (Pia) Anderson's boatyard in Stromness. This boat was so special it was exhibited by Anderson at the 1967 London Boat Show in Earl's Court.

45

BRIAN CARR and a SHIP'S PANEL, Westray

On lifting a flagstone floor in an old croft house in 2010, Brian Carr (a relative newcomer to Westray) made an extraordinary discovery. From a layer of sand, he lifted out this beautifully carved panel, well preserved in its dry tomb, and clearly a piece of decoration from a sailing ship.

According to the former director of the Norwegian Maritime Museum in Oslo, Bard Kolltveit, 'the lion carving on the panel indicates it belongs to the latter half of the 19th century, and the design resembles one which was formally approved by King Oscar in 1844. The panel has come from a Norwegian vessel...'

Westray's Linda Drever thought the panel could have been stolen, having been hidden under a flagstone floor. Following her own enquiries at the Norwegian Maritime Museum, Linda learnt that 'the shape indicates it's from the top of a ship's transom, and that the central shield indicates a date after 1847. Before that date, the lion stood on the handle of a long, curved axe, or a halberd. The oak leaves are pure ornament.'

The 'Register of Scottish Shipwrecks' was consulted by Tom Muir and, armed with only scant information, he said 'I've narrowed it down to one likely candidate. It could be the *Hortensia*, a barque which was stranded on Westray's Skea Skerries on 30th March, 1891.'

'Built in New Jersey in 1853,' Tom continued, 'the *Hortensia* was an American ship bought by the Norwegian company Pouvert and Co. of Porsgrund. The lion panel could have been added later, of course, but it's impossible to know. She was sailing from Porsgrund to Barrow-in-Furness with a cargo of boards when she was stranded off Westray in a force-10 storm. The vessel had been refloated, but was so badly damaged she was condemned as unseaworthy and sold for breaking up.'

Brian Carr's remarkable discovery is now in the hands of his friends, Linda Drever and Paul Booth, and decorates their little café near the pier at the south end of the island.

46

OLIVER DREVER and a GLASS FLOAT, Sanday

'I've been farming here for over half a century,' said Oliver Drever, at Boloquoy, his house overlooking Lashy Sound and the Calf of Eday. 'But I'm retired now… I can trace my farming ancestors here back to the early 1700s.'

Feeling that Oliver must have something interesting from the shore, I asked about his beachcombing days. Surely he'd have something, I thought. The signs were there. The sitting room was entered by first going through a large store and workshop, full of shadows, hints of sea finds. 'Nothing I can think of,' said Oliver, when I asked about any finds he might have.

But then he looked up to the top of a cupboard. 'There is something there,' he said, and I picked up a large glass float for a closer look. Brushing away a thick cloak of dust, a painting of a fine sailing ship catching the wind was revealed.

'It's a miracle the float wasn't broken on the rocks,' said Oliver. Soon after finding it, in the 1970s, he sent the float to retired seaman and artist Willie o'Neven, in North Ronaldsay. The Reverend Graham Finch, minister for both Sanday and North Ronaldsay at the time, acted as courier. So Willie applied his careful brushstrokes, and the newly decorated float was returned to a delighted Oliver.

47

SAM HARCUS and a SEA CHEST, Westray

As chief engineer on the *Grampian Defiance*, a North Sea Emergency Response and Rescue Vessel (ERRV), Sam Harcus is one of a crew of fifteen on the ship, providing standby support around North Sea oil and gas installations. Operating from Aberdeen with North Star Shipping, he works alternate four-week periods.

Photographed for this book at the Bay of Tafts near his Westray home with two of his grandchildren, Sam is holding a mahogany chest. Found by his crofter grandfather, the chest had been lost from a ship and has signs of being at one time possibly attached to a bulkhead.

When there was news that a whale had beached on Westray, when his children were small, out of curiosity Sam went to see the dead animal for himself. But, by the time he got there, the carcass had been swept away by a particularly high tide. All that was left on the sand were six of the whale's teeth, one for each of his six children. One of those teeth is held by one of Sam's grandchildren in this photograph.

48

JOHN LIPTROT and a SCOOP, Sandwick

When the 64-ton trawler *Regent Bird* ran aground on the Sandwick rocks on January 31st, 1995, the crew of four simply dropped a rope ladder over the side of the boat, walked up the shore, crossed a field and jumped into a taxi waiting for them at John Liptrot's farm. 'I remember it well,' said John. 'It was my son's fourteenth birthday, and the party with all his friends was interrupted to watch this exciting thing happening. None of the crew said a word to any of us – they just walked straight past us with their bags already packed.'

A tug was organised to tow the *Regent Bird* back into the sea. But as John and a group of friends and neighbours watched from the shore, the trawler wouldn't budge. Instead, when the tug pulled on its tow-rope, the trawler's hull cracked suddenly, bringing the operation to a sudden full-stop.

That marked the beginning of a salvaging exercise by John and the group on the shore. Some climbed on board the boat, and managed to establish a breeches-buoy system to remove most of the fish – this was sold locally and across the Pentland Firth in Scrabster. 'We kept dismantling the boat bit by bit,' said John, 'and removed radios, echo-sounders, a compass, the wheel, and the bell… everything that could be removed… it was hectic, exciting…'

Then the coastguard and the police arrived, and the frenzy around the boat suddenly stopped. An embarrassing silence descended on the scene. The police took everything away to Kirkwall (except the fish, of course), until the situation was resolved. With advice from his solicitor, John made a payment to the relevant insurance company, and all the goods were returned to him to share with his fellow salvagers.

This is a portrait of John with a souvenir, a *Regent Bird* fish scoop, on the Sandwick shore where the trawler was grounded.

49

KATE BIRKETT and a BLOCK, South Ronaldsay

Kate Birkett found this wooden disc on the shore at Newark, on South Ronaldsay's east coast, in 2012. It's a thin slice cut from the centre of a tree trunk, leaving the growth rings clearly visible. The three notches on the inner side suggested to me that the disc was something to do with engineering. It could have fitted precisely on to something and, in my ignorance, the words flange, gasket and grommet came to mind – but these things are usually made of anything but wood.

At his farm in South Ronaldsay, I asked Martin Annal about the disc (it's where I first met Kate), and he said he couldn't imagine what it was. So he volunteered to carry the disc around with him for a few days, which turned into weeks, to ask anyone he met whether they could identify it. When this plan didn't produce any answers, Martin decided to take the mystery object to Robin Duncan, who was, with his brother, the last of five generations of boatbuilders in Burray. 'It's one side of a block, part of the rigging of a sailing ship,' Duncan said, 'and the central metal plate has been lost.' There was the answer. 'And it's made of greenheart, just about the hardest wood,' Duncan continued. It's interesting that there are still parts of sailing ships being washed up on the Orkney shore.

Working part-time on Martin's farm, Kate attends to the winter byres. And she also keeps sheep and cattle, and breeds and trains sheepdogs on her own farm, which she shares with her partner, a foreman at Kirkwall's Orkney Mart. In the summer, Kate is also a tour guide when the cruise liners are at anchor.

50

FRANKIE and PEARL SINCLAIR with GLASS FLOATS, Hoy

'I used to put creels around the Flow,' said Frankie Sinclair at his cosy home on Burra Sound in Hoy, 'and, when I looked up at this stretch of coast from the boat, I used to think what a bleak-looking place; I wouldn't like to live there… I was always happy to get back to Stromness.' Feelings are a bit different now – nestled just above the shore, his home is 'a little bit of heaven,' says Frankie. Living on the island also suits Pearl, Frankie's wife, and she has recently produced a fascinating book of portraits of Hoy's residents.

Sitting at Greenhill for this photograph, Frankie is holding a glass float which was used by a Florida company for testing electronic instruments at great depths in the sea – a few have turned up on Orkney's coast in recent years. Pearl is holding a traditional glass net float, which fishermen commonly used around the British coast until around the 1940s.

The name of Frankie and Pearl's house, Greenhill, is taken from the broch next door (Orkney's like that) – it's in the background of this photograph. A satellite dish sits near the top of it today. In 1814, Walter Scott landed here, curious to see the broch, a burial mound, during his tour of the Scottish coast on the Northern Lighthouse Board's annual inspection voyage. There were a few diversions during the trip, including a visit to see Hoy's great curiosity, the Dwarfie Stane, a huge, hollowed-out boulder below the Ward Hill. Then Scott was off to Stromness, and later wrote some rude comments about the town, recording them and other observations of his journey in six diaries – later publishing them in a journal with the extraordinary title of *Northern Lights: Or, a Voyage in the Lighthouse Yacht to Nova Zembla, and the Lord Knows Where in the Summer of 1814.*

51

INGRID BUDGE and a JETSAM CAMERA, Inganess Bay

Someone mentioned Ingrid Budge to me. I could meet her in 'We Frame It' in Kirkwall. I looked at Ingrid's Facebook page first, and was fascinated by her creative approach to photography – using pinhole cameras, making photograms and lumen prints, salt prints, cyanotype and tin type, and often using old colour film, years out of date. And subjects ranging from old houses to delicate flowers.

The remarkable book of black and white photographs *Life in the Orkney Islands* by Chick Chalmers 'was instrumental in introducing me to a love of photography,' said Ingrid. 'I saw the book at my grandparents' house,' she continued, 'and they had a collection of old photographs too… the Harvest Home, and portraits… ' Soon after seeing this inspirational book, Ingrid attended Edinburgh's Napier College, where Chick was her tutor. (In 1998, Chick died in Edinburgh at the age of forty-nine.)

Much later, Ingrid studied photography again, this time at the Orkney College, and regained her interest and enthusiasm for the subject. Her photographs have an eloquent and beautiful atmosphere, and stillness.

Inganess Bay, an hour or two before sunset – a pinhole camera and a tripod, both made from pieces of driftwood, are at Ingrid's side for this portrait. And she's holding a photographic print of the shore made with this pinhole camera (a wooden box, a pinhole at one side and a piece of film at the opposite side) – it's the most elementary of cameras but, with a creative imagination, the possibilities with this camera are almost limitless.

52 MICHAEL BRASS and a WINE BARREL, Birsay

The last photograph to make this collection complete proved to be illusive for a while… just one more interesting find. The best place must be Birsay, I thought. Calling on Benny Norquoy – he's a fisherman and former attendant keeper to the Brough light – I drew a blank. But he suggested a couple of people at the Palace, but again there was nothing. I met Benny's brother too, and he said he'd had the unfortunate experience of finding a body a long time ago.

'No, there's nothing,' said a farmer in Marwick. But then added 'I did find a bust of Hitler twenty or more years ago. It was a small, wooden thing. And someone thought it might have come out of a U-boat.' The Hitler bust had been given to the TA in Kirkwall, which has its own museum. But, on enquiring, there was no trace of it.

The next day, I called on a few more farms, but without success. Then I tried Skaill Farm – nothing there, but a suggestion to try Michael Brass… 'He's on a tractor just round the corner, he's bound to have something,' I was told. 'Follow me!' said Michael, when I explained what I was looking for. He was just about to go home anyway, to a farm at the other side of the bay… On the way, alongside the road, a male hen harrier flew low over the fields, with an excited flock of starlings following at a safe distance.

The farm was clearly a beachcombing centre, I could see. There was a strange weather buoy from Canada, and a belt mounted on a board, with a round plaque inscribed 'Royal Logistics Corps'. But then Michael led the way to an old store… and in there lay a handsome barrel, found about half a century earlier by his father in a geo near their farm. 'The barrel was full of red wine when I found it,' said Freddy Brass, 'my mother enjoyed it very much… and it would have been offered to visitors too,' he added. The barrel was later used to make rhubarb champagne, and then home brew, Orkney's potent dark ale, a small part of the Orcadian culture. I'd found the perfect subject.

ENDWORD

The photographs in this volume of *Found*, as in the first, have not reflected the most common objects to be found on the islands' shores – the vast and almost infinite variety of plastic rubbish. The problem of plastic on coasts and in the oceans is a massive one, and the statistics around the issue are alarming. It's estimated that every year nearly one million seabirds, and a further one-hundred-thousand marine mammals, die from entanglement or ingestion of plastic materials in the oceans – and the problem of this toxic tide is getting worse.

A recent scientific survey revealed that pieces of plastic were found in the stomachs of 95% of dead North Sea fulmar petrels. (Fulmars are true ocean wanderers and can act as barometers, measuring the health of our seas.) And in the stomach of one dead guillemot, found on Scapa beach, there were 152 pieces of plastic.

Graphic individual examples describing other consequences of marine plastic abound. The story of the whale which was recently trapped in Scapa Flow by a discarded creel line is a distressing example of what is happening in our seas (see page 40). And, on the shore, every beachcomber will have seen dead seabirds with plastic tangled around their bodies. On Suleskerry, I saw a seal with a piece of fishing net wrapped tightly around its neck, the plastic 'rope' already cutting deeply into its flesh. (With support from another lightkeeper, we managed to cut the seal free from a slow strangulation.)

Julian Branscombe, who works for the RSPB in Orkney, commented on this tide of plastic pollution: 'I feel it defiles beaches and is an expression of our contempt for nature. The plastic we can see kills wildlife – and the plastic dust which is being produced by the power of the sea and the action of UV light could prove to be an even more serious threat.'

Others have equal concerns about the endless plastic litter on the Orkney shores (as well as in the oceans, of course). The environmental group 'Outdoor Orkney' has two initiatives concerned with the issue: one is called 'Bag the Bruck,' and has well over six-hundred volunteers who are concerned enough to remove many tons of plastic every April from almost one-hundred coastal sites around Orkney.

And another initiative is called PU3P - Pick Up 3 Pieces. It's the idea of Kirkwall teacher Lesley Mackay, who has inspired people to simply pick up three pieces of litter whenever they are outdoors in the islands. In her own school, and in other schools around Orkney, Lesley has explored the subject of litter and the plastic problem, and finds that the children she meets are horrified at the complacent attitude of so many people towards the issue.

Lesley acknowledges that the initiative is dealing with the tip of the iceberg, but that at least it is about doing something positive. 'It's also about convincing people that small groups can take action globally, and can make a difference,' she commented. 'Dealing with the problem must be about education,' Lesley continued, 'and ultimately there must be a move away from the use of plastic for so many of our needs.'

The scale of plastic pollution and its effects on the marine environment is clearly described in the 'Bag the Bruck' blog – it makes sobering reading.

Keith Allardyce